Contents

{ List of Knitting Abbreviations }

K	knit		**Inc**	increase
P	purl		**RS**	right side
KTBL	knit through back of loops		**WS**	wrong side
ST	stocking stitch, 1 row knit followed by 1 row purl		**Y/O**	yarn over
			SSK	slip 2 sts knitways, knit them together
K2tog	knit 2 together			
P2tog	purl 2 together		**Sl2tog-k1-psso**	slip 2 sts knitways on to right hand needle, knit next stitch then pass the 2 previous slipped stitches over the knitted stitch
Y F	yarn forward			
cms	centimeters			
Sl 1	slip 1			
PSSO	pass slip st over			
M1	knit into the front and back of the stitch (increase)		*** ***	refer to where a pattern is repeated within a line and is used commonly in patterns
Dec	decrease			

{ Knitting Know How }

Cable Cast On

Insert your knitting needle between the first two stitches, wrap the yarn around your needle and bring it through to the front of your work. Transfer the newly created stitch onto the left hand needle thus increasing a stitch.

Picot Edge Cast Off

Cast off 2 stitches: *Slip the 1 stitch on the right hand needle to the left hand needle. Cast on 2 stitches using the cable cast on method. Cast off 4 stitches.* Repeat from * to * until the end of the row, casting off remaining odd stitches left on the needle.

{ UK Alpaca }

UK Alpaca uses the best alpaca fleeces to make luxurious yarns that are a joy to work with. All the fleeces come from alpacas that are farmed in Britain and the yarns are processed fully worsted in the traditional mills in the north of England. One of the 'noble' fibres, alpaca is soft, luxurious, stronger and more resilient than the finest sheep's wool. It is prized for its silky feel, weightlessness and warmth.

Our undyed yarns reflect the natural fleece colour of the alpaca and come in parchment, fawn and chocolate and there is also a stunning array of dyed colours.

UK Alpaca's double knit balled yarns are in the natural and dyed shades and are 70% alpaca, 30% Bluefaced Leicester. This blend delivers a lofty yarn with no shedding. Our 4-ply yarns in the natural colours are sold on skein and cone. A second range of 4-ply, double knit and aran yarns is made from baby alpaca and merino and comes in four dyed colours and two naturals. Top of the range is a baby alpaca and silk blend, a gorgeous yarn that boasts four dyed colours and a natural parchment.

We hope you will enjoy using our yarns to knit the exciting patterns created by Monica Russel for this book.

More information and a sales page can be found on our website www.ukalpaca.com

{ Striped Gauntlets }

This is a simple pattern that would suit a knitter who is confident doing plain and purl stitches. The colours can be changed to suit your wardrobe.

Materials
- UK Alpaca D/K
- Colour A Rose One 50g ball
- Colour B Midnight blue One 50g ball
- Colour C Parchment One 50g ball

Needles
- 1 pair 4.5mm (UK 7, US 7)
- 1 tapestry needle

Tension
Using 4.5mm needles:
18 sts x 27 rows = 10mm

Please note that the yarn is used double for the cuff of the gloves only

Pattern Stitch
Rows 1 & 3: P3, *K1, Sl 1, K1, P3*, repeat to end of row.
Rows 2 & 4: *K3, P1, K1, P1*, repeat to last 3 sts K3.
Rows 5 & 7: K4, *Sl 1, K5*, repeat to last 4 sts K4.
Rows 6 & 8: P4, *K1, P5*, repeat to last 4 sts P4.

Knitting the Cuffs
C/O 39 sts with 4.5mm needles.
Row 2: KTBL to form a neat edge.
Work Pattern 8 rows once and then the first four rows once more. Cut off one of the strands of colour A and continue as follows:
Helpful hint: Twist the yarns every 2 rows so that there are no large loops.
Knit 6 rows ST using colour B.
Knit 2 rows ST using colour C.
Knit 4 rows ST using colour A.
Repeat the above 12 row sequence 2 times more.
Knit 6 rows ST using colour B then cut off this colour.
Knit 2 rows ST using colour C then cut off this colour.
Using colour A Knit 10, dec 1, Knit 16, dec 1, knit until the end of the row.

Top Rib

Row 1: With wrong side facing: *K1, P1*, repeat from * to * to last st, K1.
Row 2: *P1, K1* repeat from * to * then Purl last st.
Row 3: As row 1 of rib.
Cast of using picot cast off as follows:
Cast off 2 stitches: *Slip the 1 stitch on the right hand needle to the left hand needle. Cast on 2 stitches using the cable cast on method. Cast off 4 stitches.* Repeat from * to * until the end of the row, casting off remaining odd stitches left on the needle.

Completing the Gauntlets

From the frill end join the side seam using mattress stitch to the 3rd row down from the first blue stripe.
From the cuff end join the side seam to the top of the 2nd red stripe.
Sew in all loose ends by weaving the yarn into the seam.

{ Striped Beanie }

This hat has a snug fit and is stylish at the same time. It matches the leg warmers and fingerless gloves. The beanie will fit an average sized head.

Materials

- UK Alpaca D/K
- Colour A Rose One 50g ball
- Colour B Midnight Blue One 50g ball
- Colour C Parchment One 50g ball

Needles

- 1 pair 3.75mm (UK 9, US 5)
- 1 pair 4mm (UK 8, US 6)
- 1 tapestry needle

Tension

Using over Stocking stitch with 4mm needles
24 sts and 33 rows = 10.2mm x 10.2mm

Knitting the Hat

Using 3.75 needles and colour A, C/O 108 sts.
Row 2: KTBL to form a neat edge.
Rows 3-12: *K3, P3*, repeat from * to * until the end of the row.
Row 13: change to size 4mm needles and using yarn A increase as follows: K17 inc 1, *K15 inc 1* repeat from * to * until you have increased 6 times altogether (114 sts).
Purl 1 row.
Change to colour B: Knit 6 rows ST.

Change to colour C: Knit 2 rows ST.
Continue in set stripe pattern (remember to twist yarns every 2 rows no there are no large loops) until 2nd stripe in colour C has been completed.

Shaping (continuing stripe sequence)

Row 1: K7, *K2tog tbl, K1, K2tog, K14*, repeat from * to * x5, K2tog tbl, K1, K2 tog, K7 (102 sts).
Knit 3 rows ST.

Row 5: K6, *K2tog tbl, K1, K2tog, K12*, x5, K2tog tbl, K1, K2 tog, K6 (90 sts).
Knit 3 rows ST.
Row 9: K5, *K2tog tbl, K1, K2tog, K10*, x5, K2tog tbl, K1, K2 tog, K5 (78 sts).
Knit 3 rows ST.
Row 13: K4, *K2tog tbl, K1, K2tog, K8*, x5, K2tog tbl, K1, K2 tog, K4 (66 sts).
Knit 3 rows ST.
Row 17: K3, *K2tog tbl, K1, K2tog, K6*, x5, K2tog tbl, K1, K2 tog, K3 (54).

Row 18: Purl.
Continue to decrease as above rows on every alternative row until 18 sts are left on your needle.
End with wrong side facing.
Final row: Cut yarn leaving sufficient to sew up the side seams. Thread the yarn through the remaining sts and pull them together securing them before sewing up the side seam using a mattress stitch.
Sew in loose ends.

{ Striped Leg Warmers }

This is a simple pattern that would suit a knitter who is confident doing plain and purl stitches. The colours can be changed to suit your wardrobe.

Materials
- UK Alpaca D/K
- Colour A Rose Two 50g balls
- Colour B Midnight Blue One 50g ball
- Colour C Parchment One 50g ball

Needles
- 1 pair 5mm (UK 6, US 8) knitting needles
- 1 pair 5.5mm (UK 5, US 9) knitting needles
- 1 tapestry needle to sew in ends

Please note that the yarn is used double throughout the pattern

Knitting the Leg Warmers
Using colour A, Cast on 43 sts with 5mm needles.
Row 2: KTBL to form a neat edge.

Ankle Cuff
Row 1: *K1, P1*, repeat to last st K1.
Row 2: *P1, K1*, repeat to last st P1.
Repeat the last 2 rows 6 more times .
Change to size 5. 5 mm needles and follow pattern sequence laid out below. Remember to twist your yarn every few rows to avoid long stands at the back of your work.
Knit 4 rows ST using colour B.
Knit 2 rows ST using colour C.
Knit 4 rows ST using colour A.
Continue in set stripe, 3 more times but make the B stripe 6 rows long 3 Knit 4 rows ST colour B and 2 rows colour C. Cut off yarns B and C.
Knit 1 row using colour A. Start top of cuff (as on row 2 rib of ankle cuff).
Using set pattern (as cuff rib) repeat rows 1 and 2 five times more and row 1 one more time. Cast off stitches

Completing the Leg Warmers
Using mattress stitch, join up side seams. Sew in all loose ends by weaving them in to the side seam.

{ Diamonds are a Girl's Best Friend }

This is a really useful little scarf that will keep the chill away and look great. It is knitted from one ball or skein of 4 ply baby alpaca/silk yarn that is lovely and soft to wear. If you want a wider scarf, cast on additional stitches in multiples of 6.

Materials
- UK Alpaca 4-ply Baby Alpaca/Silk
- Ecru One 50g ball or skein

Needles
- 1 pair 4.5mm (UK 7, US 7) single pointed needles

Tension
Yarn used knits as 4ply to this tension:
Using 4.5mm needles: 18 sts x 20 rows = 10cms over stitch pattern

Knitting the Scarf
Multiples of 6 + 3.
Cast on 27 sts.
Row 1 (wrong side): Knit.
Row 2: P1, *yrn, p2tog*, rep from * to *.
Rows 3-4: Knit.
Row 5 and every WS row to 15th row: Purl.
Row 6: *K4, yf, sl 1, K1, psso*, rep from * to * to last 3 sts K3.
Row 8: K2, *K2tog, yf, k1, yf, sl 1, K1, psso, K1*, rep from * to * to last st K1.
Row 10: K1, K2tog, yf, *K3, yf, sl 1, K2tog, psso, yf*, rep from * to * to last 6 sts, K3, yf, sl 1, K1, psso, K1.
Row 12: K3, *yf, sL1, K2tog, psso, yf, K3, rep from * to end.
Row 14: As 6th row.
Row 16: Knit.
Repeat these 16 rows 20 times, repeat rows 1-3 once.
Cast off stitches.

Completing your scarf
Sew in strands of yarn from your cast on and cast off edges. Press the scarf lightly.

{ Paris Beret }

This is a pattern for a simple beret. It can be knitted in stripes or just plain.

Materials
- UK Alpaca D/K
- Colour A Damson One 50g ball
- Colour B Moss One 50g ball

Needles
- 1 pair 4mm (UK 8, US 6) single pointed needles
- 1 pair 3.25mm (UK 10, US 3)
- 1 tapestry needle

Tension
Using over Stocking stitch with 4mm needles 24 sts and 33 rows = 10.2mm x 10.2mm

Knitting the Beret
Using Yarn A double. C/O 98 sts using 3.25mm needles.
Rows 1-7: K1, P1 to end (this forms the rib).
Row 8: K1, P1 for 48 sts inc 1 stitch, rib to the end (99 sts).

From now on work with a single strand of yarn and 4mm needles. Work in 4 row stripes of each colour starting with yarn B.
Row 9: *K3 inc 1, K4 inc 1*, Repeat from * to * to end row (127 sts).
Row 10: purl.
Rows 11-20: stocking stitch.
Row 21: *K9 inc 1* repeat to last st K1, (141 sts).
Rows 22-34: ST.
Row 35: (K8, sl 1, K1, PSSO) to end K1 (127 sts).
Rows 36-42: continue in st.
Row 43: (K7 sts, sl 1, K1, PSSo) to last st K1 (113 sts).
Rows 44-46: ST.

Row 47: (K6 sts, sl 1, K1, PSSO) to last st K1 (99 sts).
Rows 48-50: ST.
Row 51: (K5, sl 1, K1, PSSO) to last st K1 (85 sts).
Rows 52-54: ST.
Row 55: (K4, sl 1, K1, PSSO) to last st K1 (71 sts).
Row 56: Purl.
Row 57: (K3, sl 1, K1, PSSO) to last st K1 (57 sts).
Row 58: Purl.
Row 59: (K2, sl 1, K1, PSSO) to last st K1 (43 sts).
Row 60: Purl.
Row 61: (K1, sl 1, K1, PSSO) to last st K1 (29 sts).
Row 62: (sl 1, P1, PSSO) to last st P1 (15 sts).

Completing the Beret
Cut wool leaving sufficient to sew up the seam. Thread a needle through the remaining stitches and pull it tightly to form centre crown and secure with a few stitches. Sew up side seam and sew in ends.

{ Highland Dreams }

This short cardigan is great with trousers, a skirt or for wearing over a dress. Colours can be adapted to match your taste and it can be made longer if you prefer simply by adding more rows before the raglan shaping. If you prefer a looser waistband omit the striped version and use the stitch worked for the cuff of the sleeves for the rib of the fronts and the back with your smaller sized needle.

Materials
- UK Alpaca D/K
- Colour A Moss x4 (5, 5, 6) balls
- Colour B Midnight Blue x2 balls
- Colour C Sapphire x2 balls
- Colour D Wine 1 (1, 1, 2) ball
- Colour E Lilac 1 (1, 1) ball
- Colour F Damson 1 (1, 2, 2) ball
- Colour G Mustard x2, (3, 3, 3) balls
- 5 (6) Buttons

Needles
- 1 pair 4.5mm (UK 7, US 7) single pointed needles (for a wider striped border use size 5mm (UK 6, US 8) needles)
- 1 pair 3.25mm (UK 10, US 3)

Tension
Over size 4.5mm needles 31 rows X 21 sts = 10cms

Sizes	Small 34-36" 86-91cm	Medium 36-38" 92-97cm	Large 40-42" 102-107cm	X Large 44-46" 112-117cm
Actual measurements	37.5" 94cm	41" 103cm	45" 115cm	50" 127cm
Sleeve to raglan shaping	17.5" 45cm	18" 46cm	19" 48cm	19" 48cm

Border Notes
I found it helpful to cut off 1 metre lengths of yarns (except colour A) and to twist colours when you change to colour A. Note the border is quite tight so check tension carefully. An alternative is to do the border in a rib, eg. K2, P2 using a size smaller needle so that it is a snug fit.

Back Border
Using 4.5mm needles and colour B, cast on 97 (109, 121, 135) stitches.
KTBL.
Cut off yarn B.
To set the coloured stripes follow the guidelines below that are shown for the smallest size and these will need to be adapted for other sizes.

Row 1: *K2A, K2D, K2A, K2E, K2A, K2F, K2A, K2G* repeat from * to * until last st, K1A.
Row 2: P1A *P2G, P2A, P2F, P2A, P2E, P2A, P2D, P2A* repeat from * to * until end of row.
Repeat rows 1 and 2 twice more.
Cut off all yarns.

Set Colour Sequence

Used after the border. You will need to incorporate the decreases and increases within it on all two tone rows to make them align.

Row 1: *K2B, K2C* Repeat from * to * until last stitch K1B.

Rows 2-5: ST colour A starting with a purl row.

Row 6: *P2B, P2C* repeat from * to * until last 3 sts, P2B, P1C.

Rows 7-10: ST colour D.

Row 11: As row 1 aligning pattern.

Rows 12-15: ST colour A, starting with a purl row.

Row 16: As row 6.

Rows 17-20: ST colour E.

Row 21: As row 1.

Rows 22-25: ST colour A, starting with a purl row.

Row 26: As row 6.

Rows 27-30: ST colour F.

Row 31: As row 1.

Rows 32-35: ST colour A, starting with a purl row.

Row 36: As row 6.

Rows 37-40: ST colour G.

This is the colour sequence for the cardigan. Each size will end on a different row.

Main Pattern

After the border work 12 rows ST using the pattern sequence above. Start with right side facing for next row.

How to increase: K2, M1, knit to last 2 sts K1, M1, K1.

Continue in ST, increasing 1 stitch at each end of the 11th row and 2 following 12th rows 103 (115, 127, 141 sts).

Continue straight until back measures 23 (24, 25, 26 cms) ending with a right side facing for the next row.

Shaping Raglan Armholes

Cast off 2 stitches at the beginning of the next 2 rows. 99 (111, 123, 137 sts).

Next row: (RS) K2, K2tog tbl, Knit to last 4 sts, K2tog, K2.

Next Row: P2, P2tog 1, (1, 1, 1) times P to last 2 (4, 4, 4) stitches, (P2tog tbl) 1, (1, 1, 1)

times, P2. 97 (107, 119, 133) stitches.
The above 2 rows shows the layout for the decreases.
Now dec 1 stitch at each end of next 1 (7, 17, 25) rows, then on every following alternate row until 35 (37, 37, 39) stitches remain.
Work 3 rows ending with RS facing for next row. Place remaining 35 (37, 37, 39) stitches on a stitch holder.

Left Front

Using 4.5mm needles and colour B, cast on 47 (53, 59, 66) stitches.
KTBL.
Cut off yarn B.
To set the coloured stripes for the border follow the guidelines below that are shown for the smallest size and will need to be adapted for other sizes.
Row 1: *K2A, K2D, K2A, K2E, K2A, K2F, K2A, K2G* repeat from * to * until last 15 sts, *K2A, K2D, K2A, K2E, K2A, K2F, K2A, K1G.
Row 2: P1G, P2A, P2F, P2A, P2E, P2A, P2D, P2A, P2G, P2A, *P2G, 2A, P2F, P2A, P2E, P2A, P2D, P2A * repeat from * to * until end of row.
Repeat rows 1 and 2 twice more.
Cut off all yarns.
Use colour sequence as for back.
Next row: Dec 1st in the middle of your row.
Work 9 rows ST.
Work increases in the same way as for the back increasing 1 stitch at the beginning of the next row and then 3 following 10th rows 50, (56, 62, 69 sts).
Continue in ST until front measures the same as the back where you have decreased for the raglan.
With right side facing, cast off 2 sts at the beginning of the next row. 48 (54, 60, 67 sts).
Purl 1 row.
Next row: (RS) K2, K2tog tbl, K to the end.
Next row: Purl to last 2 (4, 4, 4 sts), P2tog tbl 0, (1, 1, 1) times, K2.

47, (52, 58, 65) stitches.
This is the set pattern for the decreases.
Dec 1st at raglan edge of next 1, (7, 17, 25) rows then on every following alternate row until 22 (25, 25, 27) stitches remain.
Shape neck.
Next row: Wrong side. Cast off 12 (11, 11, 11) stitches. P to end.
Next row: K2, K2tog tbl, K to last 2 stitches, K2tog.
Next row: P2tog, P to end.
Small size only: Work decreases as set by the previous 2 rows x 1 (4 sts remaining).
Next row: (RS) K2, K2tog tbl (3 sts).
Next row: P2tog, K1.
Next row: K2 tog. Fasten off.
Sizes M, L and XL.
Work all decreases as with smaller size. Dec 1st at raglan armhole edge on next row and then following 2 (2, 3) alt rows **and at the same time** dec 1st at neck edge on next 3 rows and then on following 1 (1, 2) alt rows. 4 sts.
Work 1 row.
Next row: (RS) K2, K2tog tbl (3 sts).
Next row: P2tog, K1.
Next row: K2 tog. Fasten off.

Right Front

Using 4.5mm needles and colour B, cast on 47 (53, 59, 66) sts.
KTBL.
Cut off yarn B.
To set the coloured stripes follow the guidelines below that are shown for the smallest size and will need to be adapted for other sizes.
Row 1: *K2A, K2D, K2A, K2E, K2A, K2F, K2A, K2G* repeat from * to * until last 15 sts, * K2A, K2D, K2A, K2E, K2A, K2F, K2A, K1G.
Row 2: P1G, P2A, P2F, P2A, P2E, P2A, P2D, P2A, P2G, P2A, *P2G, 2A, P2F, P2A, P2E, P2A, P2D, P2A* repeat from * to * until end of row.
Repeat rows 1 and 2 twice more.

Cut off all yarns.
Use Colour sequence as for back.
Next row: Dec 1st in the middle of your row.
Work 9 rows ST.
Next row (RS): Knit until last 2 sts, M1, K2, 47 (53, 58, 66) sts.
Now following set increase pattern increase 1 ST at the end of the 3 following 10th rows. 50 (56, 62, 69) sts.
Continue straight in ST until front measures the same as the back where you have decreased for the raglan ending with a WS facing for the next row.

Shape Raglan
Cast off 2 sts at the beginning of next row and purl to end 48, (54, 60, 67) sts.
Next row: Knit to last 4 sts, K2tog, K2.
Next row: P2, P2tog, 0 (1, 1, 1) times purl to end.
Work all decreases as above and complete to match left front, reversing shapings.

Sleeves
Using colour G and 3.25mm needles cast on 43, (45, 45, 47) sts.
KTBL to form a neat edge.
Rows 1, 3, 5, 7, 9, 11: *K2, P2* repeat from * to * until last 3 stitches K2, P1.
Rows 2, 4, 6, 8, 10, 12: P1, K2 *P2, K2* repeat from * to * until end of row.
Change to 4.5mm needles.
With right side facing, starting with a knit row using row 1 of colour sequence as for the back. Work increases the same way as for the back continuing in set colour sequence.
Increase 1 st at each end of next row, and then on every following 6th row twice and then on the following 8th (8th, 6th, 6th) row until you have 67 (69, 71, 73) sts, then on every following 10th (10th, 10th, 8th) row until there are 71 (73, 75, 77) sts.
Continue straight until work measures 45 (46, 47, 47) cms ending with right side facing for next row.

Shape Raglan
Cast off 2 stitches at the beginning of the next 2 rows. 67 (69, 71, 73) stitches.
Next row (RS): K2, K2tog tbl, knit to the last 4 sts, K2tog, K2. 65 (67, 69, 71) stitches.
Next row: Purl.
Next row: Knit.
Next row: Purl.
Repeat last 4 rows 2 (2, 2, 3) more times 61 (63, 65, 65) stitches.
Working all decreases as set at the beginning and end of knit rows decrease 1st at each end of next and following alternate rows until there are 23 sts remaining.
Now decrease 1 st at each end of the following 4th row. 21 sts.
Work 1 row, ending with right side facing for next row.

Left Sleeve Only
Next row: K2, K2tog tbl, K to last 4 stitches, K2tog, K2 (19 sts).
Next row: Cast off 4 sts, Purl to end (15 sts).
Next row: Knit.
Next row: Cast off 3 sts, Purl to end (12 sts).
Next row: K2, K2tog tbl, K to end (11 sts).
Next row: Cast off 3 sts, Purl to end (8 sts).
Next row: Knit.
Next row: Purl to end.
Place 5 sts on a stitch holder.

Right Sleeve Only
Next row: Cast off 5 sts, K to last 4 sts, K2tog, K2.
Next row: Purl.
Next row: Cast off 3 stitches, knit to end (12 sts).
Next row: Purl.
Next row: Cast off 3 stitches, K to last 4 stitches, K2tog, K2 (8sts).
Next row: Purl.
Next row: Cast off 3 stitches, knit to end (5 stitches).
Next row: Purl.
Place stitches on a holder.

Work to match button band, adding 5 (5, 6, 6) buttonholes evenly spaced up the band, ending with a right side facing for the next row.

To make buttonhole: Pattern 3, cast off 2 stitches, pattern to end. On the next row, cast on 2 stitches over the cast off stitches and pattern to the end.
Sew buttonhole band onto right hand front.

Collar

With right side facing and 3.25mm needles knit across the 8 sts of the buttonhole in set rib, then pick up and knit 15 (17, 17, 19) stitches up right hand side of neck, now pick up and knit 10 sts from the top of the right sleeve before the stitches on holder.
Knit 5 stitches on holder.
Knit the 35 (37, 37, 39) from the stitch holder decreasing 4 stitches evenly across them.
Knit 5 stitches from stitch holder.
Knit 10 sts from left hand sleeve.
Knit 14 sts down left side of neck.
Knit the 8 sts from the stitch holder (continuing this part in set stitch of the button band), 106, (112, 112, 118) stitches.
Next: Work 4 rows in set pattern as used in button band section, ending with the wrong side facing for the next row.
Next 2 rows: Cast off 5 stitches at the beginning of each row.
Continue in set pattern until work measures 10cms ending your knitting on the wrong side. With the right side of your work facing, cast off stitches.

Completing your Cardigan

Sew in all loose ends by weaving them into the rear of your pieces.
Press each piece of your cardigan carefully.
Join the raglan seams with right sides facing using a mattress stitch. Use the stripes to ensure that the seams are evenly matched.
Join the side seams and straight edge of the sleeves.

Button Band

Using 3.25mm needles and colour G cast on 8 sts.
KTBL.
Row 1: *K2, P2* repeat from * to *.
Row 2: *P2, K2* repeat from * to *.
Continue rows 1 and 2 until the button band fits up the left front opening to the shaping for the neck when it is slightly stretched. End with right side facing for the next row. Put stitches on a stitch holder. Sew band to front using a slip stitch.

Band for Buttonhole

Using 3.25mm needles and colour G cast on 8 sts.
KTBL.
Row 1: *K2, P2* repeat from * to *.
Row 2: *P2, K2* repeat from * to *.

{ Heather Beanie }

This beanie is unisex and will keep you beautifully warm on a winter's day. The colours featured were inspired by a recent trip to Scotland but they can easily be changed to suit your personal taste. The beanie co-ordinates with the Heather mittens.

Materials

- UK Alpaca D/K
- Colour A Moss Green One 50g ball
- Colour B Damson One 50g ball
- Colour C Mustard One 50g ball

Needles

- 1 pair 3.75 (UK 9, US 5) single pointed needles
- 1 pair 4mm (UK 6, US 8) single pointed needles
- 1 tapestry needle

Tension

Over 4mm needles
27 rows x 22 sts = 10 x 10cm (4 x 4in)

Knitting the Beanie

Using size 3.75 needles and colour A cast on 108 sts.
Rows 1-10: ST colour A.
Rows 11-14: change to colour B and *k1, p1* repeat from * to * until end of row.
Change to size 4mm needles.
Rows 15-16: ST colour C.
Row 17: *K3A, K3C* repeat from * to *.
Row 18: *P1A, P1C, P1A, P1C, P1B, P1C.
Row 19: as row 17.
Rows 20-21: ST colour C starting with a purl row.
Row 22-25: ST colour B, starting with a purl row.
Rows 26-29: ST colour A, starting with a purl row.
Rows 30-31: ST colour C, starting with a purl row.
Row 32: *P3C, P3A* repeat from * to *.
Row 33: *K1C, K1B, K1C, K1A, K1C, K1A* repeat from * to * until end of row.
Row 34: As row 3⒉
Rows 35-36: ST colour C.
Rows 37-40: ST colour A.
Row 41-44: ST colour B.
Rows 45-47: As rows 17-19.
Row 48: Purl colour C.

Decreasing

Row 1: using colour C: K4, *SS, K1, PSSO, K9* repeat from * to * to the last 3 sts, knit (98 sts). *SS K1 PSSO then* *(all rows)*
Row 2: Purl using colour B.
Row 3: using colour B: Knit 4, *SS, K1, PSSO, K8* repeat from * to * until last 2 sts, K2 (88 sts).
Row 4: Purl using colour B.
Row 5: using colour B: Knit 4 *SS, K1, PSSO, K7* rep from * to * until last st, K1 (78 sts).
Row 6: Purl using colour A.
Row 7: using colour A: K4 *SS, K1, PSSO, K6* rep from * to * (68 sts).
Row 8: Purl using colour A.
Row 9: using colour A: K4, *SS, K1, PSSO, K5* rep from * to * until last 6 sts K4, SS, K1, PSSO (58sts).
Row 10: Purl using colour C.
Row 11: using colour C: K4, *SS, K1, PSSO, K3* rep from * to * until last st K1 (47 sts).
Row 12: Purl using colour C.
Row 13: using colour C: K4, *SS, K1, PSSO, K2* rep from * to * (35 sts).
Row 14: Purl using colour B.
Row 15: K1, *SS, K1, PSSO, K1* rep from * to *.

Completing the Beanie

Thread your tapestry needle through remaining stitches and draw them together securing the top of the beanie. Now sew up the side seam using a mattress stitch with right sides facing.

{ Heather Mittens }

These are classical mittens knitted in Scottish heathery colours. They accompany the beanie hat knitted in the same colours.

Materials
- UK Alpaca D/K
- Colour A Moss One 50g ball
- Colour B Damson One 50g ball
- Colour C Mustard One 50g ball

Needles
- 1 pair 4mm (UK 6, US 8) single pointed needles

Tension
Over 4mm needles
27 rows X 22 sts = 10 x 10cm (4 x 4in)

Right Hand

Using 4mm needles cast on 40 stitches in colour A.
KTBL.
Row 1: *K1, P1* repeat to end of row (right side).
Work 19 more rows in rib ending with a WS row.

Shaping for the thumb

Row 21-22: ST colour B.
Row 23: Using colour B K20, M1, K5, M1, K15 (42 sts).
Row 24: Purl colour B.
Rows 25-26: ST colour C.
Row 27: K20, M1, K7, M1, K15 (at the same time, K1C* K3A, K3C* repeat until last stitch K1A (44 sts).
Row 28: P1C, *P1A, P1C, P1A, P1C, P1B, P1C* repeat from * to * until last stitch, P1A.
Row 29: As row 27 following the colour

sequence without the increases.
Row 30: Purl colour C.
Row 31: Using colour C, K20, M1, K9 M1, K15 (46 sts). Cut off yarn C.
Rows 32-34: ST colour B starting with a purl row.
Row 35: Using colour B, K20, M1, K11, M1, K15 (48 sts).
Rows 36: Purl colour A.
Rows 37-38: ST colour A.

Divide For Thumb

Next row (RS): K33 colour A turn.
Next row: P13 colour C. Now working on these 13 sts only knit 12 rows ST as follows.
Row 1: K colour C.
Row 2: P3C, P3A, P3C, P3A, P1C.
Row 3: *K1A, K1C, K1B, K1C, K1A, K1C* repeat from * to * once more then K1A.
Row 4: As row 2.
Rows 5 and 6: ST colour C.

Rows 7-10: ST colour A. Cut off yarn A.

Rows 11-12: ST colour B.

Row 13: Using colour B, K1, sl 1, K1, PSSO, knit to last 3 sts, sl 1, K1, PSSO. K1 (11 sts).

Row 14: Purl colour B. Cut off yarn B.

Repeat rows 13 and 14 twice more using colour C.

Cut off yarn leaving a sufficient length to sew up thumb seam. Sew in all loose ends by weaving them into the back of your work. Thread your tapestry needle with your cut off length of yarn and place your stitches onto it. Draw up the stitches at the top of the thumb and stitch it together before sewing up side seam of the thumb using a mattress stitch with right sides facing.

Now rejoin yarn with right side facing and knit picking up 2 stitches from the base of the thumb, then knit to end of row. (37 sts).

Next row purl colour C.

ST next 20 rows in colours/pattern as follows:

Row 1: Knit colour C.

Row 2: *P3A, P3C* repeat from * to * until last stitch P1A.

Row 3: K1C*, K1A, K1C, K1A, K1C, K1B, K1C*, repeat from * to * until end of row.

Row 4: As row 2.

Rows 5-6: ST colour C.

Rows 7-10: ST colour A.

Rows 11-14: ST colour B.

Rows 15-16: ST colour C.

Row 17: K1C, *k3A, k3C* repeat from * to *.

Row 18: *P1A, P1C, P1A, P1C, P1B, P1C* repeat from * to * until last stitch P1A.

Row 19: As row 17.

Row 20: Purl colour C.

Next row: Using colour C K1, K2tog, K14, K2tog, knit to last 3 stitches, K2tog, K1 (34 sts) Cut off yarn C.

Next row: Purl using colour B.

Next row: Using colour B, K1, K2tog, Knit to last 3 sts, K2tog, K1,(32 sts).

Next row: Purl using colour B.

Repeat last 2 rows twice more the first one in colour C and then the remaining ones in colour A (28 sts).

Next row: K1, K2tog, *K2, K2tog* repeat from * to * until last stitch K1.

Cut off a piece of yarn that will be sufficiently long to thread it though the remaining stitches and sew up your side seam with right sides facing using a mattress stitch.

Left Hand

Work as for right hand until the shaping of the thumb.

Row 21-22: ST colour B.

Row 23: Using colour B K15, M1, K5 M1, K20 (42 sts).

Row 24: Purl colour B.

Rows 25-26: ST colour C.

Row 27: K15, M1, K7, M1, K20 (at the same time, K1C* K3A, K3C* repeat until last stitch, K1A (44 sts).

Row 28: P1C *P1A, P1C, P1A, P1C, P1B, P1C* repeat from * to * until last stitch, P1A.

Rows 29: As row 27 following colour sequence without the increasing of stitches.

Row 30: Purl colour C.

Row 31: Using colour C, K15, M1, K9, M1, K20 (46 sts). Cut off yarn C.

Rows 32-34: ST colour B starting with a purl row.

Row 35: Using colour B, K15, M1, K11, M1, K20 (48 sts).

Rows 36: Purl colour A.

Rows 37-38: ST colour A.

Divide For Thumb

Next row (RS): K28 colour A turn.

Next row: P13 colour C. Now continue working as right hand.

Re join colour A. With right side facing, pick up 2 stitches from the base of the thumb, then knit to end of row. (37 sts).

Next row: purl using colour C

Continue knitting as for right hand.

Complete your left mitten as you did for the right hand.

{ Simple Snood }

This is an easy snood to make, as you only need to be able to cast on, cast off and knit. Choose a colour and knit a versatile item to add to your winter wardrobe. If you prefer a scarf simply buy more yarn and knit a longer version.

Materials
- UK Alpaca D/K Parchment
- Two 50g balls

Measurements and sizes
The snood can be made narrower and longer.
Width: 30cms
Length: 68cm (34cm when folded for the snood).

Needles
- 1 pair 4mm (UK 8, US 6) single-pointed needles
- 1 pair 4.5mm (UK 7, US 7) single-pointed needles

Instructions
Using 4.5mm needles cast on 39 sts.
Change to 4mm needles.
Knit 1 row.
Rows 1-2: *K1, wrap yarn around needles (from right side to wrong side) K2 tog*
rep from * to * until end of row.
Rows 3-8: Knit.
Repeat the 8 row pattern until you have used up nearly all your yarn, ending the last sequence with knit 4 rows.
Cast off sts.

Completion
With right sides facing join both ends of the snood together using a mattress stitch.

{ Two Tone Beanie Hat } & Baby Booties

These are two patterns to make simple bootees and a matching hat. Both are fun to make and will keep your baby toasty warm. Try making them in alternate colour ways to suit your taste.

Materials
- UK Alpaca D/K
- Colour A Sapphire One 50g ball
- Colour B Grey One (Two) 50g balls

Sizes
Newborn, 3, 6, 12 months

Needles
- One pair 4.5mm (UK 7, US 7) single pointed needles

Knitting the Bootees

Using 4.5mm needles and colour A, Cast on 27 (31, 35, 39) sts.
Rows 1 & 2: Knit.
Row 3: K1, M1, K12 (14, 16, 18) sts M1, K1, M1, K12, (14, 16, 18) sts M1, K1 (31, 35, 39, 43) sts on needle.
Row 4 and all even rows: Knit.
Row 5: K2, M1, K12 (14, 16, 18) sts M1, K3, M1, K12, M1, K2 (35, 39, 43, 47 sts).
Row 7: K14, (16, 18, 20) K2tog, K3, K2tog, K14, (16, 18, 20).
Row 9: K14, (16, 18, 20) K2tog, K1, K2tog, K14, (16, 18, 20) (31, 35, 39, 43 sts).
Row 11: K13, (15, 17, 19 sts) K2tog, K1, K2tog, K13, (15, 17, 19 sts) (29, 33, 37, 41 sts).
Row 13: K12, (14, 16, 18 sts), K2tog, K1, K2tog, K12, (14, 16, 18 sts) (27, 31, 35, 39 sts).

Row 15: K11 (13, 15, 17 sts), K2tog, K1, K2tog, K11 (13, 15, 17 sts).
Row 17: K10, (12, 14, 16 sts) K2tog, K1, K2tog, K10, (12, 14, 16 sts).
Row 19: K9, (11, 13, 15 sts), K2tog, K1, K2tog, K9, (11, 13, 15 sts).
Row 20: knit, cut off yarn A for 1st size – join in yarn B.
Row 21: Sizes 2, 3 and 4 only: K10, (12, 14), K2tog, K1, K2tog, K10, (12, 14 sts).
Row 22: Knit: Cut off yarn A for 2nd size. Join in yarn B.
Row 23: Sizes 3 & 4 only: K11, (13), K2tog, K1, K2tog, K11, (13).
Row 24: Knit Cut off yarn A for 3rd size. Join in Yarn B.
Row 25: Largest size only. K12, K2tog, K1, K2tog, K12.
Rows 21 (23, 25, 27) - **36** (38, 38, 42) Knit in colour B.

Cast off using the picot method as follows: Cast off 2 stitches: *Slip the 1 stitch on the right hand needle to the left hand needle. Cast on 2 stitches using the cable cast on method. Cast off 4 stitches.* Repeat from * to * until the end of the row, casting off remaining odd stitches left on the needle.

Making up the Bootees

Using a mattress stitch with right side facing join up sole seam. Join rear seam with a mattress stitch. Fold the cuff (colour B) in half and join up to the fold using a mattress stitch. (There will be a flap open at the rear).

Knitting the Baby Beanie Hat with Tie

Using Colour B and 4.5mm (UK 7; US 7) needles Cast on 56 (62, 68, 68) sts.
Knit 14, (14, 16, 16) rows.
Purl 1 row – cut off yarn B.
Purl 2 rows colour A.
Continue in ST until hat measures 8 (10, 12, 14cms) from colour change.
Decreasing for crown.
All even numbered rows are purl.
Row 1: K1st, *k2tog, k7 (8, 9, 9) sts* repeat from * to * k1.
Rows 2 - 4: st.
Row 5: K1, *k2tog, k6 (7, 8, 8) sts* repeat from * to * until last st k1.
Row 7: K1, *k2tog, k5 (6, 7, 7) sts* repeat from * to * until last st k1.
Row 9: K1, *k2tog, k4 (5, 6, 6) sts* repeat from * to * until last st k1.
Row 11: K1, *k2tog, k3 (4, 5, 5) sts* repeat from * to * until last st k1.
Row 13: K1, *k2tog, k2 (3, 4, 4) sts* repeat from * to * until last st k1.

Row 15: K1, *k2tog, k1 (2, 3, 3) sts* repeat from * to * until last st k1.
Continue decreasing in this way until you have 20 sts on needle.
Row 19: Cut off yarn B. Join yarn A. All sizes K1, *k2tog* rep to last st k1 (10 sts).
Row 20: purl.

Ties

Working on 1st 5 sts only:
Knit until tie measures 6cms.
Next row: K2tog, K1, K2tog.
Next row: Knit.
Next row: K2tog, k1.
Next row: Knit.
Next row: Cast off st.
Repeat the above to make 2nd tie.

Making up the Baby Beanie Hat with Tie

Sew in loose ends by weaving them in to the rear of work.
Sew up seam with right sides facing using a mattress stitch until you get to the turn up which is sewn up on the reverse side using a mattress stitch. Turn up the rim.
Tie the ties into a knot.

{ Striped Baby Raglan Cardigan, } Hat & Bootees

This raglan sleeved cardigan has been knitted in classical stripes with a simple border to add a unique twist. It is a unisex pattern and can be knitted in colours of your choice.

Materials
- UK Alpaca D/K
- Colour A Sapphire x 1 (2) balls
- Colour B: Parchment x 1 ball

Sizes
Newborn, 3-6 months, 6-12 months, 12-18 months
- Length: 20, 22, 25, 28 cms
- Width: 22, 24, 26, 29 cms
- Sleeve length: 21, 24, 27, 30 cms

Needles
- 1 pair 4mm (UK 8; US 6)
- 1 pair 4.5mm (UK 7; US 7) single pointed needles)
- 5 (6) buttons

Tension
Using 4.5mm needles:
18sts x 27 rows = 10mm

Tension
Using 4.5mm needles:
18 sts x 27 rows = 10mm

Knitting the Cardigan

Back
Using 4mm and colour A needles C/O 46, (50, 54, 60) sts.
KTBL.
Row 1: *K2A, K2B* repeat from * to * until end of row.
Row 2: *P2B, P2* repeat from * to * until end of row (note this sequence is for all sizes and there should be alternate coloured squares.
Rows 3 and 4: As rows 1 and 2.
Change to 4.5mm needles.
Continue in ST working 4 rows colour A , 4 rows colour B until work measures 11, 13, 15, 17 cms.
Shape Armholes.
Cast off 2 sts at the beginning of the next 2 rows.
Now decrease 2 sts every other row as follows:
K1, K2tog knit to last 3 sts S1, K1, PSSO, K1 until 16, 18, 20, 22 sts remain on your needle.
Purl 1 row. Place remaining sts on a stitch holder.

Right Front
C/O 23, (25, 27, 30) sts, using 4mm needles. Work same pattern sequence as the back until work measures 11, (13, 15, 17) cms. Cast off 2 sts on armhole edge, then continue decreasing every other row on the last 3 sts of a knit row (Sl 1, K1, PSSO, K1) until work measures 17, 19, 22, 25 cms then whilst continuing raglan decrease also cast off for the neckline as follows:
0-3 months and 3-6months: 3 stitches every 2 rows x 2, then 2 sts x 1.
6-12 months and 12-18 months: 3 sts alternate rows x 2 then 2 sts alternate rows x 2.
Cast off remaining stitches.

Left Front

Work left side as right side reversing shaping, and decreasing by K1, K2tog.

Sleeves -both alike

C/O 28 (30, 32, 34 sts) using 4mm needles. KTBL.

Rows 1-4: Same pattern sequence as the back. Change to 4.5mm needles and work stripes as for the back.

Increasing: On next and following 6th (6th, 8th, 8th) increase one st at either end until there are 34 (38, 40, 44) sts.

Work straight until sleeve measures 10 (12, 15, 18 cms).

C/Off 1 st either end and then decrease for the raglan as you did for the back until 8, (10, 10, 10) sts remain. Cast off sts.

Making up your cardigan

Press all pieces of knitting.

Sew raglans, sides and undersides of sleeves matching your stripes.

Neckline border

With right side facing you and 4mm needles pick up 16 (17, 18,19) sts then the 16, (18, 20, 22) sts from the stitch holder and then the 16 (17, 18, 19) sts from the other side of the front. Knit 3 rows in K2, P2 pattern as you did for the borders. Using colour A cast off sts.

Buttonhole border

Left or right side depending on preference. Using colour A pick up sts evenly down the front of the cardigan.

Next row: *K2, P2* repeat to end.

Next row: make 5 (5, 6, 6) buttonholes spacing them evenly down the border whilst working rib sequence. To make a simple buttonhole: K2tog, Y/O.

Next row: knit rib sequence.

Cast off sts.

Sew on buttons.

Now sew in all loose ends by weaving them into the rear of your cardigan.

Baby Hat

Using Colour A and 4.5mm (UK 7;US 7) needles Cast on 56 (62, 68, 68) sts.

Knit 14, (14, 16, 16) rows .

Purl 3 rows.

Continue in ST until hat measures 8, (10, 12, 14cms) from colour change.

Decreasing for crown.

All even numbered rows are purl.

Decreasing for crown.

All even numbered rows are purl.

Row 1: K1st, *k2tog, k7 (8, 9, 9) sts* repeat from * to * k1.

Rows 2-4: st.

Row 5: K1, *k2tog , k6 (7, 8, 8) sts* repeat from * to * until last st k1.

Row 7: K1, *k2tog , k5 (6, 7, 7) sts* repeat from * to * until last st k1.

Row 9: K1, *k2tog , k4 (5, 6, 6) sts* repeat from * to * until last st k1.

Row 11: K1, *k2tog , k3 (4, 5, 5) sts* repeat from * to * until last st k1.

Row 13: K1, *k2tog , k2 (3, 4, 4) sts* repeat from * to * until last st k1.

Row 15: K1, *k2tog , k1 (2, 3, 3) sts* repeat from * to * until last st k1.

Continue decreasing in this way until you have 20 sts on needle.

Row 19: *k2tog * repeat from * to * until end of row (10sts).

Row 20: purl.

Cut off yarn A.

Join in yarn B.

Ties

Working on 1st 5 sts only:

Knit 4 rows.

Next row: K2tog, K1, K2tog.

Next row: Knit.

Next row: K2tog, k1.

Next row: Knit.

Next row: Cast off st.

Repeat the above to make 2nd tie.

Making up the Baby Hat

Sew in loose ends by weaving them into the rear of work.

Sew up seam using a mattress st.

Join the flaps together by winding your yarn around them twice and then fastening it off.

Sew a button in the centre of your flaps.

Knitting the Bootees

Using 4.5mm needles and colour A, Cast on 27 (31, 35, 39) sts.

Rows 1 & 2: Knit.

Row 3: K1, M1, K12 (14, 16, 18) sts M1, K1, M1, K12, (14, 16, 18) sts M1, K1 (31, 35, 39, 43) sts on needle.

Row 4 and all even rows: Knit.

Row 5: K2, M1, K12 (14, 16, 18) sts M1, K3, M1, K12, (14, 16, 18) sts) M1, K2 (35, 39, 43,47 sts).

Row 7: K14, (16, 18, 20) K2tog, K3, K2tog, K14 ,(16, 18, 20).

Row 9: K14, (16, 18, 20) K2tog, K1, K2tog, K14, (16, 18, 20) (31, 35, 39, 43 sts).

Row 11: K13, (15, 17, 19 sts) K2tog, K1, K2tog, K13, (15, 17, 19 sts) (29, 33, 37, 41 sts).

Row 13: K12, (14, 16, 18 sts), K2tog, K1, K2tog, K12, (14, 16, 18 sts) (27, 31, 35,39 sts).

Row 15: K11 (13, 15, 17 sts), K2tog, K1, K2tog, K11 (13, 15, 17 sts).

Row17: K10, (12, 14, 16 sts) K2tog, K1, K2tog, K10, (12, 14, 16 sts).

Row 19: K9, (11, 13, 15 sts), K2tog, K1, K2tog, K9, (11, 13, 15 sts).

Row 21: Sizes 2, 3 and 4 only: K10, (12, 14), K2tog, K1, K2tog, K10, (12, 14 sts).

Row 22: Knit .

Row 23: Sizes 3 & 4 only: K11, (13), K2tog, K1, K2tog, : K11, (13).

Row 24: Knit Cut off yarn A for 3rd size.

Join in Yarn B.

Row 25: Largest size only. K12, K2tog, K1, K2tog, K12.

Row 21: (23, 25, 27) Knit 10, (11, 12, 13) sts, then knit twice (knit 1 as normal, then transfer st to left hand needle and knit it again) then knit remaining sts on your needle. Knit a further 8 (10, 12, 14) rows on the first 11 (12, 13, 14) sts. Change to yarn B, Knit 1 row. Cast off using the picot method as follows: Cast off 2 stitches: *Slip the 1 stitch on the right hand needle to the left hand needle. Cast on 2 stitches using the cable cast on method. Cast off 4 stitches.* Repeat from * to * until the end of the row, casting off remaining odd stitches left on the needle.

Now do the same with the sts remaining on your needle. This forms the front divider in the bootee.

Making up the Bootee

Using a mattress stitch with right side facing join up sole seam. Join rear seam with a mattress stitch. Fold the cuff (colour B) in half and join up to the fold using a mattress stitch, (there will be a flap open at the front of the bootee).

Sew a button in between the slit at the front. Sew in all loose ends by weaving them into the rear of your work.

{ Beanie Hat & Stripy Shoes }

These patterns make simple baby shoes and a matching hat. Both are fun to knit and will keep your baby lovely and warm. Try making them in alternative colour ways to suit your taste.

Materials
- UK Alpaca D/K
- Colour A Midnight Blue One 50g (two) balls
- Colour B Parchment One 50g ball

Sizes
Hat: Newborn, 3, 6, 9-12 months
Baby shoes: Newborn, 3, 6, 9-12 months

Needles
- 4.5mm (UK 7, US 7) single pointed needles

Tension
Using 4.5mm needles: 18 sts x 27 rows = 10mm

Knitting the Bootees
Using 4.5mm needles and colour A, Cast on 27 (31, 35,) sts.
Rows 1 & 2: Knit.
Row 3: K1, M1, K12 (14, 16,) sts M1, K1, M1, K12, (14, 16) sts M1, K1 (31, 35, 39) sts on needle.
Row 4 and all even rows: Knit.
Row 5: K2, M1, K12 (14, 16) sts M1, K3, M1, K12 (14, 16), M1, K2 (35, 39, 43) sts.
After row 6 change to colour B and them change colours every 2 row.
Rows 7-10: (10, 12) Knit.
Row 11 or (13): K11 (13, 14), *sl 1, K1, psso*, from * to * x3, (4 for largest size only) K1, *K2tog* from * to * x3, (4 for largest 2 sizes only) K11, (13, 14).
Row 12: Knit.
Cast off sts.
For largest size only: knit 2 more rows.
Cast off sts.

Making The Strap
Cast on 10 (12, 12) sts.
KTBL.
Cast off sts.

Completing the Bootees
Using a mattress stitch with right side facing join up sole seam. Join rear seam with a mattress stitch. Sew strap on to shoe about 1/3 of the way towards the heel.
Add an embellishment of a button or pom pom to make the shoe more fun.

Knitting the Stripy Beanie Hat

Using Colour A and 4.5mm (UK 7; US 7)
needles Cast on 56 (62, 68) sts.
Knit 14 (14, 16) rows.

Purl 3 rows. Now join in yarn B and continue
to work in Stocking stitch with 2 stripes of
each colour until hat measures 8 (10, 11 cms)
from colour change.

Decreasing for crown.

All even numbered rows are purl.

Row 1: K1st, *k2tog, k7 (8, 9) sts* repeat
from * to * k1.

Rows 2-4: st.

Row 5: K1, *k2tog, k6 (7, 8) sts* repeat from
* to * until last st k1.

Row 7: K1, *k2tog, k5 (6, 7) sts* repeat from
* to * until last st k1.

Row 9: K1, *k2tog, k4 (5, 6) sts* repeat from
* to * until last st k1.

Row 11: K1, *k2tog, k3 (4, 5) sts* repeat from
* to * until last st k1.

Row 13: K1, *k2tog, k2 (3, 4) sts* repeat
from * to * until last st k1.

Row 15: K1, *k2tog, k1 (2, 3) sts* repeat
from * to * until last st k1.

Continue decreasing in this way and purling
the even numbered row until you have 20 sts
remaining ending with a purl row.

Next row: *K2 tog* repeat from * to * until
end of the row.

Next row: purl.

Cut off yarn leaving a sufficient length to
draw a tapestry needle through the remain sts
and to sew up side seam.

Completing the Stripy Beanie Hat

Sew in loose ends by weaving them into the
rear of work. Sew up seam using a mattress
stitch with right sides facing. Join the turn
up using a mattress stitch and wrong sides
facing. Sew in all loose pieces of yarn.

{ Patterned Baby Cardigan, Bootees & Pixie Hat }

This is a versatile unisex baby cardigan that is knitted in a range of colours that blend well together. The pattern is simple as is knitted in a stocking stitch. I have made the hat and bootees in colours of my choice that complement the cardigan.

Materials
• UK Alpaca D/K
• Colour A Moss One 50g ball
• Colour B Midnight Blue One 50g ball
• Colour C Sapphire One 50g ball
• Colour D Wine One 50g ball
• Colour E Lilac One 50g ball
• Colour F Damson One 50g (Two) balls
• Colour G Mustard One 50g ball
• 6 (7) Buttons

Sizes
Newborn, 3-6 months, 6-12 months, 12-18 months
• Length: 20, 23, 26, 29 cms
• Width: 22, 24, 26, 29 cms
• Sleeve length: 12, 15, 18, 21 cms

Needles
• 1 pair 4.5mm (UK 7, US 7) single pointed needles

Tension
Using 4.5mm needles: 18 sts x 27 rows = 10mm

Knitting the Cardigan

Back
Using 4.5mm needles and colour A Cast on 42 (46, 50, 56) sts.
KTBL.
Work 2 rows in a K2, P2 rib.
Row 3: *K2B, K2C* repeat from * to * until last 2 sts K2B.
Rows 4-7: Using colour D, ST starting with a purl row. Cut off yarn D.
Row 8: *P2B, P2C * repeat from * to * until last 2 sts P2.
Rows 9-12: ST Colour A.
Row 13: as row 3.
Rows 14-17: ST colour E, starting with a purl row. Cut off yarn E.
Row 18: As row 8.
Rows 19-22: As rows 9-12.
Row 23: As row 3.
Rows 24-27: ST colour F, starting with a purl row. Cut off yarn F.
Row 28: As row 8.
Rows 29-32: As rows 9-12.
Row 33: As row 3.
Row 34-37: Using colour G, ST starting with a purl row. Cut off yarn G.
Row 38: As row 8.
This is the set colour sequence for the cardigan and is repeated until you reach the required measurements. Note for the 1st size only you will decrease for the armhole before row 34.

Armholes
When work measures 11 (13, 15, 17) cms, cast off 1st either side. Note after the decrease, rows 3 and 8 pattern repeat will start with K1, (P1) and end with K1 (P1) due to the decreased stitch for armholes.
Continue in set colour sequence until work measures 20 (23, 26, 29) cms. Cast off stitches.

Left Front

Note: Match sts on dot lines as you start each row after the armhole decrease.

Cast on 23 (25, 27, 30) sts.

Work as back until work measures 11 (13, 15, 17) cms. Cast off 1 st on the left hand side for the armhole. At the same time decrease (K2tog) 1 stitch on the 2nd stitch from the edge every 3 (3, 4, 4) rows on the right hand side for the neckline until you have 15 (16, 17, 19) sts left on your needle.

Continue to knit straight until the front measures the same as the back. Cast off sts. Note the decrease should be done 2 sts from the edge.

Right Front

Make buttonholes. These are done simultaneously with your knitting as follows: Cast off 1 st, 2 sts from the edge then make up the st by YF. Space buttonholes: 1 cm from cast on edge and then 2 (2, 3,3) more 5 (6, 5, 5.5) cms apart.

Work as left side until work measures 11 (13, 15, 17) cms. Reverse shapings for the armhole and front and when decreasing use K1 (P1), Sl 1, PSSO method. (2 sts from edge).

Sleeves

Cast on 28 (30, 32, 34) sts.

KTBL.

Work 2 rows in a K2, P2 rib.

Continue working in set pattern increase 1 stitch on either side every 10 (10, 12, 12) rows until you have 34 (38, 42, 46) sts on your needle until work measures 12 (15, 18, 21) cms. Cast off sts.

Making up the Cardigan

Sew the shoulder seams, the sides and the undersides of sleeves using a mattress stitch using the stripes to help you sew seams evenly. Sew buttons along the front edge matching the spaces for the buttonholes.

Pixie Hat

Using colour G and 4.5mm needles cast on 56 (62, 68, 68) sts.

KTBL.

Row 1: *K1, P1* repeat from * to * until end of row.

Continue in rib for another 3 rows.

Change to colour E.

Continue in ST until hat measures 8 (10, 12, 14) cms from colour change.

Decreasing for crown.

All even numbered rows are purl.

Row 1: K1st, *k2tog, k7 (8, 9, 9) sts* repeat from * to * k1.

Rows 2-4: st.

Row 5: K1, *k2tog, k6 (7, 8, 8) sts* repeat from * to * until last st k1.

Row 7: K1, *k2tog, k5 (6, 7, 7) sts* repeat from * to * until last st k1.

Row 9: K1, *k2tog, k4 (5, 6, 6) sts* repeat from * to * until last st k1.

Row 11: K1, *k2tog, k3 (4, 5, 5) sts* repeat from * to * until last st k1.

Row 13: K1, *k2tog, k2 (3, 4, 4) sts* repeat from * to * until last st k1.

Row 15: K1, *k2tog, k1 (2, 3, 3) sts* repeat from * to * until last st k1.

Continue decreasing in this way until you have 20 sts on needle.

Row 19: *k2tog* repeat from * to * until end of row (10 sts).

Row 20: purl.

Cut off yarn E.

Ties

Working on 1st 5 sts only:

Knit 4 rows.

Next row: K2tog, K1, K2tog.

Next row: Knit.

Next row: K2tog, k1.

Next row: Knit.

Next row: Cast off st.

Repeat the above to make 2nd tie.

Making up the Pixie Hat

Sew in loose ends by weaving them into the rear of work.

Sew up seam using a mattress st.

Join the flaps together by winding your yarn around them twice and then fastening it off.

Sew a button in the centre of your flaps.

Bootees

Using 4.5mm needles and colour A, Cast on 27 (31, 35, 39) sts.

Rows 1 & 2: Knit.

Row 3: K1, M1, K12 (14, 16, 18) sts M1, K1, M1, K12 (14, 16, 18) sts M1, K1 (31, 35, 39, 43) sts on needle.

Row 4 and all even rows: Knit.

Row 5: K2, M1, K12 (14, 16, 18) sts M1, K3, M1, K12 (14, 16, 18) sts, M1, K2 (35, 39, 43, 47 sts).

Row 7: K14 (16, 18, 20) K2tog, K3, K2tog, K14 (16, 18, 20).

Row 9: K14 (16, 18, 20) K2tog, K1, K2tog, K14 (16, 18, 20) (31, 35, 39 43) sts.

Row 11: K13, (15, 17, 19) sts, K2tog, K1, K2tog, K13 (15, 17, 19) sts (29, 33, 37, 41 sts).

Row 13: K12 (14, 16, 18 sts), K2tog, K1, K2tog, K12 (14, 16, 18) sts (27, 31, 35, 39 sts).

Row 15: K11 (13, 15, 17 sts), K2tog, K1, K2tog, K11 (13, 15, 17) sts.

Row 17: K10 (12, 14, 16 sts), K2tog, K1, K2tog, K10 (12, 14, 16) sts.

Row 19: K9 (11, 13, 15) sts, K2tog, K1, K2tog, K9 (11, 13, 15) sts.

Row 20: knit, cut off yarn A for 1st size – join in yarn B.

Row 21: Sizes 2, 3 and 4 only: K10 (12, 14), K2tog, K1, K2tog, K10 (12, 14) sts.

Row 22: Knit: Cut off yarn A for 2nd size. Join in yarn B.

Row 23: Sizes 3 & 4 only: K11 (13), K2tog, K1, K2tog, K11 (13).

Row 24: Knit. Cut off yarn A for 3rd size. Join in Yarn B.

Row 25: Largest size only. K12, K2tog, K1, K2tog, K12.

Row 21 (23, 25, 27): Knit 10 (11, 12, 13) sts, then knit twice (knit 1 as normal, then transfer st to left hand needle and knit it again) then knit remaining sts on your needle. Knit a further 8 (10, 12, 14) rows on the first 11 (12, 13, 14) sts. Cast these sts off. Now do the same with the sts remaining on your needle. This forms the front divider in the bootee.

Making up the Bootees

Using a mattress stitch with right sides facing join up sole seam. Join rear seam with a mattress stitch. Fold the cuff (colour B) in half and join up to the fold using a mattress stitch, (there will be a flap open at the front of the bootee).

Sew a button in between the slit at the front.

Sew in all loose ends by weaving them into the back of your work.

{ Fair Isle Headband }

This headband is knitted using a simple Fair Isle pattern.

Materials
- UK Alpaca DK
- Colour A Parchment or Midnight blue One 50g ball
- Colour B Rose or Mustard One 50g ball
- Colour C Grey or Wine One 50g ball
- Colour D Jade One 50g ball

Needles
- 1 pair 4mm (UK 8, US 6) single pointed needles
- 1 pair 4.5mm (UK 7, US 7) single pointed needles

Tension
21 sts x 27 rows = 10cms over ST using 4.5mm needles

Knitting the Headband
C/O 105 sts using 4mm needles and colour A.
Row 1: *K3, P3* repeat to last 3 sts, K3.
Row 2: *P3, K3* repeat to last 3 sts, P3.
Row 3: Knit.
Row 4: Purl.
Change to 4.5mm needles.
Row 5: Start working from the chart (row 1), increasing 3 sts evenly across the row (108 sts). Work 19 rows from the chart, note the pattern is repeated 9 times.

Change to 4mm needles.
Dec 3 sts evenly across next row.
Row 24: Purl.
Row 25: Knit.
Row 27: *P3, K3* repeat to last 3 sts P3.
Row 28: *K3, P3* repeat to last 3 sts K3.
Cast off sts.

Making Up the Headband
Press item.
Sew in loose ends of yarn. Using a mattress st join side seams.

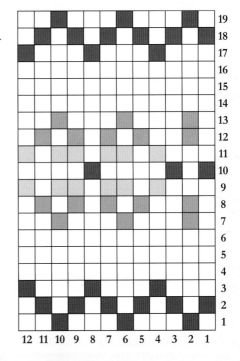

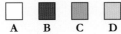

{ Fair Isle Wrist Cuffs }

These pretty wrist cuffs will keep you warm on chilly days and yet enable you to use your fingers freely.

Materials
- UK Alpaca DK
- Colour A Midnight Blue or Parchment One 50g ball
- Colour B Mustard or Rose One 50g ball
- Colour C Wine or Silver Grey One 50g ball
- Colour D Jade One 50g ball

Needles
- 4mm (UK 8, US 6) single pointed needles
- 4.5mm (UK 7, US 7) single pointed needles

Tension
21 sts x 27 rows = 10cms over ST using 4.5mm needles

Knitting the Wrist Cuffs

Using 4mm needles and colour A, C/O 42 sts KTBL.

Row 1: *K1, P1* repeat to end of row.

Row 2: *K1, incl P1, (K1, P1 x3)* repeat from * until end of row (47 sts).

Row 3: Change to 4.5mm needles and knit 1 row increasing 3 sts evenly across your sts (50 sts).

Rows 4-6: ST starting with a purl row.

Row 7: Start working from the grid; Note you repeat the pattern 4 times and then the first 2 sts again. Continue until you have completed all 19 rows.

Row 26: Purl.

Row 27: K3, dec 1, K12 decl, K12 decl, K12 decl, K3 (46 sts).

Row 28: Purl.

Rows 29-36: Follow chart from rows 7-14 The pattern is repeated 3 times and then the first 10 sts once more.

Row 37: K4, decl, *K10 decl* repeat until last 4 sts knit (42 sts).

Row 38: Purl.

Rows 39-41: follow chart rows 1-3. The pattern is repeated 3 times and the first 8 sts again.

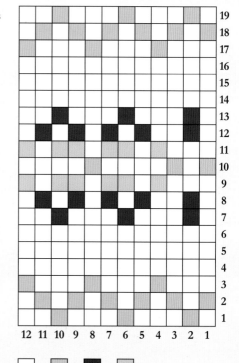

A   B   C   D

46

Row 42: P1, P2tog, P 17, P2tog, P17, P2tog, P1 (39 sts).
Row 43: Change to 4mm needles *K1, P1* repeat from * to * until last st K1.
Row 44: *P1, K1* repeat to last st P1.
Row 45: as row 43.
Row 46: Cast off sts.

Making up the Wrist Cuffs

Sew up side seams leaving a space for the thumb.
Note the wider rib is the base of the glove.
Sew in all loose ends by weaving them into the rear of the glove.

{ Fair Isle Beanie }

This is a pattern for a Beanie made in the Fair Isle style. Fair Isle knitting originated on the remote island of Fair Isle that lies midway between the Orkney and Shetland Islands.

Materials
• UK Alpaca DK
• Colour A Midnight blue or Parchment One 50g ball
• Colour B Mustard or Rose One 50g ball
• Colour C Wine or Silver Grey One 50g ball
• Colour D Jade One 50g ball

Needles
• 4mm (UK 8, US 6) single pointed needles
• 4.5mm (UK 7, US 7) single pointed needles

Tension
21 sts x 27 rows over ST using a 4.5 needle

Knitting the Hat

C/O 100 sts using 4mm needles and colour A. Knit into the back of the sts to form a neat edge.
Rows 1-7: *K2, P2*, repeat to end.
Row 8: Using rib as set knit to the end decreasing 1 st in the middle of the row (99 sts). Change to 4.5mm needles.
Note: Odd rows on the grids are knit and even row numbers are purl.

Row 9: *K3, inc 1, K4 inc 1*, repeat from * to * until last st K1 (127 sts).
Rows 10-12: Stocking st.
Rows 13 (grid row 1) - 18: Start using grid from row 1.
Row 19: Using grid (row 7) and working from right to left and colours A and C work in increases whilst incorporating the pattern. *K 9, inc 1* to last st K1 (141 sts) 11 pattern repeats and the first 9 sts again.

Rows 20-31: follow instructions from grid until row 19 of grid pattern.

Row 32: Purl.

Row 33: *K8, SL, K1, PSSO*, repeat to last stitch K1 (127 sts).

Row 34: Purl.

Rows 35-41: follow the grid from rows 7-13 repeating the pattern 10 times and then the first 7 sts again.

Row 42: Purl.

Row 43: *K7, S1, K1, PSSO*, repeat from * to * K1 (113 sts).

Row 44: Purl.

Rows 45-47: Using grid work rows 1-3.

Row 48: Purl.

Row 49: *K6, S1, K1, PSSO*, to last st K1 (99 sts).

Row 50: Purl.

Row 51: Using grid row 17 follow pattern with colour C and at the same time *K5, S1, K1, PSSO*, repeat from * to * (85 sts) Note the colour sequence should match the chart when taking the decreases into the pattern.

Row 52-53: ST follow chart rows 18 & 19.

Row 54: Purl.

Row 55: Using Colour A only *K4, S1, K1 PSSO*, repeat from * to * until last st K1.

Row 56: Purl (71 sts) Cut off yarn D.

Row 57: Using colour B Follow grid row 1 and at the same time *K3, SL1, K1 Psso* repeat from * to * last St K1. Note the colour

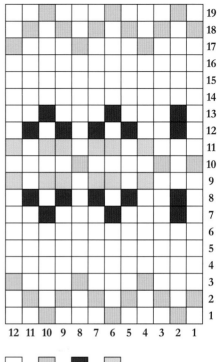

12	11	10	9	8	7	6	5	4	3	2	1	

A   B   C   D

sequence should match the chart when taking the decreases into the pattern K1. (57 sts).

Row 58-59: Follow rows 2-3 of chart St starting with a purl row. Cut off yarn B.

Row 60: using colour A *P2, S1, P1, PSSO*, repeat from * to * to last st P1 (43 sts).

Row 61: using colour A *K1, S1, K1, PSSO*, repeat to last st K1 (29 sts).

Row 62: *P1, S1, P1, PSS0*, repeat to last st P1.

Making up your Beanie

Cut yarn leaving sufficient to sew up side seams. Thread your tapestry needle with a length of yarn and take it through the remaining sts on your knitting needle. Draw sts up tightly to form the crown of the hat. Sew up side seams using a mattress stitch and match the patterns.

Sew in all loose ends.

{ City Headband }

This headband comes in two versions, one in black (the narrow one), and one in white. Both of the versions can have optional bows that may either be sewn or pinned on, in your choice of colours.

Materials
- UK Alpaca DK
- Colour A Black One 50g ball
- Colour B Parchment One 50g ball

Needles
- 1 pair 4mm (UK 8, US 6) single pointed needles for version A
- 1 pair 4.5mm (UK 7, US 7) single pointed needles for version B
- 1 cable needle

Measurements
- Width narrow headband: 8cms
- Width wide headband: 10cms

Knitting the Headband

Using 4mm (4.5mm) needles cast on 28 (30) sts. KTBL.

Row 1: K1A, (K2B), *work right crossover on 4 sts as follows: slip 2 sts onto cable needle and hold at back of work, K2 then K2 from cable needle*, repeat from * to * until last 3 sts (4 sts) K3 (A), (K4B).

Row 2 and all even numbered rows: K1A, (K2B) purl to last st, (2 sts) K1A, (K2B).

Row 3: K3 (K4B), *work left crossover on 4 sts as follows: Slip 2 sts on to cable needle and hold at front of work, K2, then K2 from cable needle*, repeat from * to * until the last 1st, (sts) k1A, (k2B).

Continue repeating rows 1-4 until the headband fits neatly around your head when slightly stretched ending with a row 4 of the pattern. As a guideline I have knitted it until it measures 46cms.

Cast off sts.

Bow x 2 halves

C/O 13 sts.

Making the bow – this can be done in black or white.

Cast on 13 sts.

KTBL.

Row 1: RS p2, (k1, p1) 4 times, k1, p2.

Row 2: *K2, (p1, k1) 4 times, p1, k2.

Rows 3-4: Repeat rows 1 and 2.

Row 5: P2, k1, p1, ssk, k1, k2tog, p1, k1, p2.

Row 6: K2, p1, k1, p3, k1, p1, k2.

Row 7: P2, k1, p1, sl2tog-k1-psso, p1, k1, p2.

Row 8: K2, (p1, k1) twice, p1, k2.

Row 9: P2, ssk, k1, k2tog, p2.

Row 10: K2, p3, k2.

Row 11: P2, sl next 3 sts onto a cable needle, wrap yarn round it twice, knit sts from cable needle, p2.

Row 12: K2, p3, k2.

Cut off yarn.

On the first half of the bow, thread a tapestry needle with the end of the yarn and draw it through your remaining sts, pull it tightly.

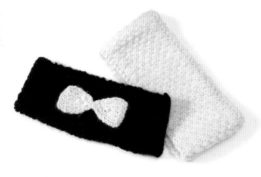

On the second part of the bow, take the yarn already used on the first half and draw it through the sts left on your needle so that the right sides are facing each other. Draw up all the sts and wrap your wool around the centre twice. Fasten off yarn.

Making Up Your Headband

With right sides facing use a mattress st to join the seams of the headband. Sew in all loose ends to the rear of your work.
Sew or pin the bow on to the headband to add a pretty detail.

{ Ooh La La }

This is a very versatile black and white wrist cuff. If you prefer you can knit it in one colour but I like 'the Channel look'. The textured main body offsets the flouncy edge.

Materials

- UK Alpaca DK
- Colour A Parchment One 50g ball
- Colour B Black One 50g ball

Needles

- 4mm (UK 6, US 8) single pointed needles
- 4.5mm (UK 7, US 7) single pointed needles
- 1 cable needle

Bell border

Using 3.75mm needles and Colour A cast on 52 sts.
KTBL.
Row 1: RS *p2, (k1, p1) 4 times, k1*, p2 repeat from * to *.
Row 2: *K2, (p1, k1) 4 times, p1, k2*, repeat from * to * until end of row.
Rows 3-4: Repeat rows 1 and 2.
Row 5: *P2, k1, p1, ssk, k1, k2tog, p1, k1, p2*, repeat from * to * to end of row (44 sts).
Row 6: *K2, p1, k1, p3, k1, p1, k2*, rep from * to * until end of row.
Row 7: *P2, k1, p1, sl2tog-k1-psso, p1, k1, p2*, repeat from * to * until end of row (36 sts).
Row 8: *K2, (p1, k1) twice, p1, k2*, repeat from * to * until end of row.
Row 9: *P2, ssk, k1, k2tog, p2*, repeat from * to * until end of row (28 sts).
Row 10: *K2, p3, k2*, repeat from * to * until end of row.
Row 11: *P2, sl next 3 sts onto a cable needle, wrap yarn round it twice, knit sts from cable needle, p2*, repeat from * to * until end of row.
Row 12: *K2, p3, k2*, repeat from * to * until end of row.
Cut off yarn A and join in yarn B.
Change to 4mm Needles.

Main Body

Next row: K4, inc 1, *k1, inc 1*, repeat from * to * until last 3 sts knit (38 sts).
Special Note: Knit the yarn over loops.
Row 1 (wrong side): K3, *p1 (y/o, p1) 3 times k3*, repeat from * to * until end of row (53 sts).
Row 2: *p3, k7*, repeat from * to * until last 3 sts, p3.
Row 3: K3, *p1, (p2tog, p1) twice, k3*, repeat from * to * until end of row (43 sts).
Row 4: *p3, k5*, repeat from * to * until last 3 sts, p3.
Row 5: K3, *p2, p2tog, p1, k3*, repeat from * to * until end of row (38 sts).
Row 6: *p3, k4*, repeat from * to * until last 3 sts, p3.
Row 7: Knit.
Row 8: Purl.
Repeat the above 8 rows 4 more times - note the last pattern repeat of rows 7 and 8 should be done with 3.75 needles.
Cast off sts using 3.75mm needles.

Completing the Wrist Cuffs

Join side seams using a mattress st with right sides facing. Leave the frill open and join 4.5cms from the wrist end (cast on edge) and 5cms from finger the end.
Sew in all loose pieces of yarn by weaving them into the rear of your cuff.

{ Ruched Boot Cuff }

This boot cuff that will insulate and add style to a pair of boots whether they are smart leather ones or Wellingtons. The pattern is in a classic black and white but it could equally be knitted in subtle colours.

. . . .

Materials
• UK Alpaca DK
• Colour A Black One 50g ball
• Colour B Parchment One 50g ball

Needles
• 1 pair 5mm (UK 6, US 8) single pointed needles

Special Knitters Notes
All yarn is used double for this item.

To knit the vertical stripes after the first row you may find it easier to knit the knit stitches through the back of the stitch and slip the purl stitches from the back.

. . . .

Knitting the Boot Cuffs

Make 2.
Using 5mm needles and colour A cast on 53 sts.
Row 1: *K1, P1* repeat from * to * until last st K1.
Row 2: P1, *K1, P1* repeat from * to * until end of row.
Rows 3-20: as rows 1 and 2.

Pattern Section

Row 1: (Right side) Using colour B, (k1, sl 1) 5 times; *k12, sl 1, (k1, sl 1) 4 times. Repeat from * to * once more to last st, k1.
Row 2: Using colour B, (p1, sl 1) 5 times, *P 12, sl 1, (p1, sl 1) 4 times; repeat from * to * once more to last st, p1.
Row 3: Using colour A, k2, sl 1, (p1, sl 1) 3 times; *k14, sl 1, (k1, sl 1) 3 times. Repeat from * to * once more to last 2 sts, k2.
Row 4: Using colour A, p2, sl 1, (p1, sl 1), 3 times; repeat from * to * once more to last 2 sts, p2.
Repeat rows 1-4 of pattern 5 more times.
Cut off yarn B.
Knit 1 row colour A.
Cast off using picot method.

Completing the Boot Cuff

Sew in loose ends by weaving them into sts at the rear of your work. With right sides facing use a mattress stitch to join the side seams of the pattern component of the boot cuff.
Join up the rib component of the cuff using a mattress st with wrong sides facing.

{ Damson & Moss Wrist Cuffs }

Cosy and pretty, these wrist warmers are a beautiful addition to your wardrobe.
Note yarn is used double throughout the pattern.

Materials
- UK Alpaca DK
- Moss or Damson Two 50g balls
- 1.2m ribbon

Needles
- 4.5mm (UK 7, US 7) single pointed needles

Size
These are one size
Length 15cms

Tension
26 rows and 16.2 sts per 10cm over Lace Stitch using yarn double and 4.5mm needles

Hills and Valley Lace Stitch
Work with a multiple of 13 sts.

Rows 1 & 3: Moss stitch (*K1, P1* repeat to end of row).

Rows 2 & 4: Moss Stitch (*P1, K1* repeat to end of row).

Row 5: P3, *SS, K1, PSSO, K3, YO, K1, YO, K3, K2tog, P2*, repeat from * to * ending last repeat with P3.

Rows 6, 8, 10 and 12: Purl.

Row 7: P3, *SS, K1, PSSO, K2, YO, K3, YO, K2, K2tog, P2*, repeat from * to * ending

the last repeat with P3.

Row 9: P3, *SS, K1, PSSO, K1, YO, K2tog, YO, K1, YO, SS, K1, PSSO, YO, K1, K2tog, P2*, ending last repeat with P3.

Row 11: P3, *SS, K1, PSSO, YO, K2tog, YO, K3, YO, SS, K1, PSSO, YO, K2tog, P2*, repeat from * to * ending the last repeat with P3.

Note: Both wrist warmers and are knitted identically.

Knitting the Wrist Warmers
C/O 32 sts with size 4.5mm.

Row 2: KTBL.

Start Hills and Valley Pattern.

Row: Start working from Hills and Valley instructions decreasing 2 sts in the first row only, (30 sts).

Complete the 12 rows of the pattern three times and then the first 4 rows once more.

Row 43: *K1, P1* repeat to the end of row
Repeat row 43 two more times.
Cast off sts.

Completing the Wrist warmers
With right sides facing use a mattress stitch to join side seams. 5cms from the top and 6cms from the wrist end Sew in any loose ends by weaving them into your knitting.

{ The Lacy Hat that can be a Snood or a Cowl }

This is a clever hat that can easily be converted into a snood or cowl simply by undoing the tie. I have used a lace stitch to add interest and texture to the design. You can use either plaited wool, a pretty cord or ribbon to make the tie at the top of the hat.

Note yarn is used double throughout the pattern.

Materials
- UK Alpaca DK
- Moss or Damson Three 50g balls
- 1.2m ribbon or cord

Needles
- 3.5 (US 4) single pointed needles
- 4.5mm (UK 7, US 7) single pointed needles

Tension
26 rows and 16.2 sts per 10cm over Lace Stitch using yarn double and 4.5mm needles

Hills and Valley Lace Stitch

Work with a multiple of 13 sts.
Rows 1-4: Moss stitch *K1, P1* repeat to last st K1.
Row 5: P3, *SS, K1, PSSO, K3, YO, K1, YO, K3, K2tog, P2*, repeat from * to * ending last repeat with P3.
Rows 6, 8, 10 and 12: Purl.
Row 7: P3, *SS, K1,PSSO, K2, YO, K3, YO, K2, K2tog, P2*, repeat from * to * ending the last repeat with P3.
Row 9: P3, *SS, K1, PSSO, K1, YO, K2tog, YO, K1, YO, SS, K1, PSSO, YO, K1 K2tog, P2* ending last repeat with P3.
Row 11: P3, *SS, K1, PSSO, YO, K2tog, YO, K3, YO, SS, K1, PSSO, YO, K2tog, P2*, repeat from * to * ending the last repeat with P3.

Hat or Snood

Using 3.5mm needles C/O 94sts.
Next row KTBL.
Row 1: *K2, P2* repeat to last 2 sts K2.
Row 2: *P2, K2* repeat to last 2 sts P2.

Repeat the above 2 rows 4 more times increasing 1 st in the middle of the 10th row
Change to size 4.5mm needles.

Start Hills and Valley Lace Stitch

Complete the 12 rows of the pattern four times. On **row 1** of the 5th pattern repeat you will insert spaces for the ribbon as follows: *K1, P1, K1, P1, K2tog, yfwd, * repeat to last 5 sts K1, P1, K2tog, yfwd, K1.
Rows 2-12: continue from rows 2-12 of Hills and valley lace stitch.
Next 2 rows: *K1, P1* repeat to end of row. Cast off sts. Cut yarn leaving sufficient to join up your side seam.

Completing the Hat or Snood

With right sides facing use a mattress stitch to join the side seams. Sew in any loose ends by weaving them into your knitting. Take your ribbon/cord and weave it in and out of the spaces you created. Draw up the ribbon and make a bow for the hat or tie it loosely for the snood.

{ Five Fingered Gloves }

These are like very old fashioned fingerless gloves knitted in a modern yarn. They are perfect for cycling, gardening and going for walks with the dog as they leave your fingers free.

Materials
- UK Alpaca DK
- Mustard Two 50g balls

Needles
- 4mm (UK 8, US 6) single pointed needles
- 4.5mm (UK 7, US 7) single pointed needles

Tension over Stocking Stitch
20 sts = 10cm
28 rows = 10cms

Right Glove
Cast on 38 ST using 4mm needles.
Row 1 (RS): K2, *P2, K2* rep from * to * to end.
Row 2: P2, *K2, P2* rep from * to * to end
Repeat rows 1 and 2 until work measures 11cms ending with a RS row to start st.
Change to 4.5mm needles.
Knit 4 rows ST.

Shape Gusset for Thumb
Row 1: K18, inc in next st, K2, inc in next st, K to end (40 sts).
Knit 3 rows ST (starting with a purl row).
Row 5: K18, inc in next st, K4, inc in next st, K to end (42 sts).
Knit 3 rows ST (starting with a purl row).
Row 9: K18, inc in next st, K6, inc in next st, K to end (44 sts).
Knit 3 rows ST (starting with a purl row).
Row 13: K18, inc in next st, K8, inc in next

st, K to end (46 sts).
Knit 3 rows ST (starting with a purl row).

Shape Thumb
Row 1: (RS) K30 and turn.
Row 2: P11, turn, and cast on 2 sts.
Row 3: Cast on 2 sts and knit a further 11 sts (13 sts).
Rows 4-5: ST on these 13 sts.
Row 6: *K1, P1* repeat from * to * K1.
Row 7: *P1, K1* repeat from * to * P1.
Cast off sts and sew up thumb seam.

Shape Hand
Return to your sts at the bottom of the thumb and with right side facing pick up and knit 2 sts from the base of the thumb, knit to end (37 sts).
Work 11 rows ST starting with a purl row and ending with RS facing for next row.

Shape 1st Finger

Row 1: with right side facing K25, turn.
Row 2: P11, turn.
Row 3: Cast on 2 sts and knit another 11 sts (13 sts).
Rows 4-5: ST 13 sts on needle.
Row 6: *K1, P1* repeat from * to * K1.
Row 7: *P1, K1* repeat from * to * P1.
Cast off sts and sew up seam.

Shape 2nd Finger

Row 1: With right side facing return to sts at base of 1st finger and pick up 2 sts, K4 and turn.
Row 2: P11, turn.
Rows 3 Cast on 2 sts and knit another 11 sts.
Rows 4-5: ST 13 sts on needle.
Row 6: * K1, P1 * repeat from * to * K1.
Row 7: * P1, K1 * repeat from * to * P1.
Cast off sts and sew up seam.

Shape 3rd Finger

Row 1: With right side facing return to sts at base of 2nd finger and pick up 2 sts, K4 and turn.
**Row 2: P11, turn.
Row 3: Cast on 2 sts and knit a further 11 sts (13 sts).
Rows 4-5: ST on these 13 sts.
Row 7: *K1, P1* repeat from * to * K1.
Row 8: *P1, K1* repeat from * to * P1.
Cast off sts and sew up seam.

Shape 4th Finger

Row 1: With right side facing return to sts at base of 3rd finger and pick up 3 sts, knit to end (11 sts).
Rows 2-4: ST.
Row 6: *K1, P1* repeat from * to * K1.
Row 7: *P1, K1* repeat from * to * P1.
Cast off sts and sew up side seam of your glove.**

Left Glove

Follow instructions for right glove to beginning of thumb gusset shaping.

Shape Thumb Gusset

Row 1: K15, inc in next st, K2 inc in next st, K to end (40 sts).
Knit 3 rows st starting with a Purl row.
Row 5: K15, inc in next st, K4 inc in next st, K to end (42 sts).
Knit 3 rows st starting with a Purl row.
Row 9: K15, inc in next st, K6 inc in next st, K to end (44 sts).
Knit 3 rows st starting with a Purl row.
Row 13: K15, inc in next st, K8 inc in next st, K to end (46 sts).
Knit 3 rows st starting with a Purl row.

Shape Thumb

Row 1: (RS) K27, turn.
Row 2: P11, turn.
Row 3: Cast on 2 sts and knit another 11 sts (13 sts).

Rows 4-5: ST on these 13 sts.
Row 6: *K1, P1* repeat from * to * K1.
Row 7: *P1, K1* repeat from * to * P1.
Cast off sts and sew up thumb seam.

Shape Hand

Return to sts at the base of the thumb and
with right side facing pick up and knit 2 sts
from the base of thumb, K to end (37 sts). K
11 rows with RS facing for next row.

Shape First Finger

Row 1: K23 and turn.
Row 2: P11, turn.
Row 3: Cast on 2 sts and knit another 11 sts.
Rows 4-5: rows ST on these 13 sts.
Row 6: *K1, P1* repeat from * to * K1.
Row 7: *P1, K1* repeat from * to * P1.
Cast off sts and sew up seam.

Shape 2nd Finger

Row 1: Return to sts at base of 1st finger,
and, with right side facing pick up and knit
2 sts from the base of the 1st finger, K5 and
turn.
Row 2: P11 and turn.
Row 3: Cast on 2 sts and knit another 11 sts
(13 sts).
Rows 4-5: ST on these 13 sts.
Row 6: *K1, P1* repeat from * to * K1.
Row 7: *P1, K1* repeat from * to * P1.
Cast off sts and sew up seam.

Shape 3rd Finger

Row 1: Return to sts at base of 2nd finger,
and, with right side facing, pick up and knit
2 sts from the base of the 2nd finger, K4 and
turn.
Complete as instructions for right glove from
**.

Completing the Gloves

Sew in all loose ends and press garment
lightly.

{ Comfy Hat }

This is a great hat for fighting off the winter chill. The hat is suitable for confident knitters. It will fit an average sized head but can be adapted for all sizes by increasing or decreasing the number of stitches or the needle size.

Materials
UK Alpaca D/K
Two 50g balls

Needles
1 Pair 4.5mm (UK 7, US 7)
1 Pair 5mm (UK 6, US 8)
1 tapestry needle

Please note that the yarn is used double throughout the pattern

Knitting the Hat
Knotted Rib.
Cast on 88 sts.
Row 2: KTBL.
Rows 3-8: *K1, P1*, repeat from * to * until end of row.
Row 9: K1, P1, *K3 sts into next st by knitting from loop, then back loop, then front loop, P1*, repeat from * to * until end of row.
Row 10: K1, *P3 sts tog as 1, K1*, repeat from * to * until end of row.
Change to 5mm needles.
Begin main pattern as follows, note the pattern is worked in multiples of 8:
Row 1: *K1, P3*, repeat from * to * until the end of the row.
Row 2: *K1, P5, K1, P1*, repeat from * to * until end of row.
Row 3: K2, *P1, K3*, repeat from * to last 2 sts P1, K1.
Row 4: P2, *K1, P1, K1, P5*, repeat from * to * until last 6 sts K1, P1, K1, P3.
Repeat the last 4 rows 5 times more and then rows 1-3 once more.
Decreasing for the crown.
Row 28: *K1, P1, K1, P1, P2tog, P2*, repeat

from * to * (77 sts).
Row 29: Knit.
Row 30: *K6, K2tog*, repeat from * to * until last 5 sts Knit. (68 sts).
Row 31: Knit.
Row 32: *K4, K2tog*, repeat until last 2 sts, K2 (57 sts).
Row 33: Knit.
Row 34: *K3, K2tog*, repeat until last 2 sts, K2 (46 sts).
Row 35: Knit.
Row 36: *K2, K2tog*, repeat until last 2 sts, K2 (35 sts).
Row 37: Knit.
Row 38: *K1, K2tog*, repeat until last 2 sts, K2 (24 sts).
Row 39: Knit.

Completing Hat
Cut yarn leaving sufficient yarn to draw needle through remaining loops and to sew the side seam.
Thread yarn through remaining stitches on the needle. Gather up the loops and fasten securely, then join the side seam using a mattress stitch.
Complete your hat by sewing in loose ends.

{ Alpacas ~ an Introduction }

Alpacas are members of the South American Camelid family along with the guanaco, llama and vicuna. Their traditional keepers are the Aymara and Quechua people of the high Andes. They used selective breeding to develop the llama as a beast of burden, and the alpaca for its high quality fleece.

Worldwide the alpaca population is estimated to be 3 million, with the majority in the South American regions of Peru, Chile and Bolivia. Today the alpaca is farmed not only in South America, but also in North America, Canada, Australia, New Zealand and most of the countries of Europe. In Britain there are around 35,000 alpacas.

Alpacas are bred for their fibre and so the quality of that fibre is extremely important. Breeders in Britain and the rest of the world

are trying to produce alpacas with uniform fine dense fleeces that will give them the maximum return. Alpacas are shorn every summer once the frosts are past and most will clip between two and three kilos.

Alpacas are lovable and endearing animals that are a pleasure to be around and to work with. Their docile nature and natural